Msomaji's
MAGIC
Carpet

Paris

Illustrated by: Rachel Gadson • Written by: Tiffany D. Smith

Book copyright © 2020 Tiffany Dionne Smith,
The Love of Food & Travel LLC. All rights reserved.

Library of Congress Cataloging-in-Publication Data
Msomaji's Magic Carpet by Tiffany Smith

Library of Congress Control Number: 2021902752

ISBN: 978-0-578-85480-9

Preface

This book is more than just a reminder about the importance of providing the gift of travel to children from low income households. This book is also spiritual. It is about the power of the written and spoken word, visualization, meditation and—most importantly—faith.

I declare that this book will change the lives of millions of little boys and girls who think that their dreams are out of reach. This book is for young people all around the world with curious, talented minds who believe that opportunities only stretch as far as their immediate neighborhoods.

May they be inspired to go further than the block. May they go as far as Creation, The Ancestors and their imaginations can carry them.

Ase'!

This is Msomaji. She lives on the South Side of Chicago with her mom, dad and two sisters. She likes playing video games and listening to music, but her favorite hobby is learning all about travel. Whether she is reading a book, visiting a museum, watching a TV show, or eating at a restaurant, she is always eager to learn more about the world.

Msomaji dreams of one day getting on a plane and visiting every state and every country, tasting new foods and learning about the history of people from other lands. Right now though, all she can do is dream because her parents can't afford to take her on a trip.

"Watching a movie, Mama?" Msomaji asked as she walked into the living room and sat on the arm of the sofa.

"Yes, baby. Some old European film," her mom replied.

"So when can we go there? I wanna see Paris!" Msomaji excitedly pointed at the screen.

"I wish we could, sweetie. But you know that we just had the baby, and Mama isn't working right now."

"One day, I'm gonna see the Eiffel Tower up close," Msomaji said. "I'm gonna wear a black beret and a pretty red dress with red shoes! I'm gonna eat French food and drink from a fancy glass with my pinky up like this." Msomaji pretended to sip from a glass while holding her pinky in the air.

Her dad stood at the window with his back turned and listened as Msomaji talked about her love of food and travel. It hurt him that his job cooking at the hotel barely paid him enough to feed his family, but he always encouraged Msomaji to dream.

He gathered himself so that Msomaji couldn't see that he was upset. Then he turned, looked her in the eyes and said, "You and your sisters are the three most important people in my life, and I love you very much. I wish that I could take you to Paris, but someday you'll go. Continue to *dream big, kid*."

Msomaji was a little disappointed, but she knew that her parents loved her and were doing the best that they could do.

"Okay, daddy," Msomaji replied, reaching out to give him a big hug and kiss. "Goodnight, Mama!" Msomaji ran upstairs to her room, sat on her bed, and picked up the baby blanket that her dad had someone make for her when she was born. It was white with red lace trim and her name was embroidered in red cursive in the middle. Every night before she went to sleep, she would imagine that her blanket was a *magic carpet* that could take her wherever she wanted to go.

This nightly ritual gave Msomaji so much joy. That night, she was determined to see Paris. She sat on her magic carpet, closed her eyes, took a deep

breath, and imagined herself experiencing all of the cool things she'd read about Paris—watching the Eiffel Tower light up at night, visiting the Mona Lisa at the Louvre Museum and tracing the footsteps of historical Black figures. She roamed the neighborhood where the famous author *James Baldwin* lived, strolled the Avenue de Champs-Elysees where *Josephine Baker* performed, and sailed the banks of the Seine River where musician *Miles Davis* dined.

The next morning, she was awakened by her mother yelling her name. "Wake up, Msomaji or you'll be late for school!"

Msomaji opened her eyes, remembered Paris and smiled. She was excited because her seventh grade class was going on a field trip to an African American History museum and she couldn't wait to find something new to discover. "Okay, Mom! I'm headed downstairs," she yelled.

Msomaji showered, got dressed, and put on a pair of jeans and her favorite sweater. It was black with sparkly letters that spelled out 'Paris' on the front.

She ran downstairs, gave her mom a hug and a kiss, grabbed the cinnamon-raisin bagel that was wrapped up for her in aluminum foil and dashed out the door.

"Be blessed! Have a great day at school," her mom yelled.

"Okay, Mama! I will!" Msomaji jumped on the school bus and quickly found a window seat. She couldn't wait to get to the museum.

Her best friend, Michelle, hopped on the bus and sat next to her. "Hey Msomaji," she said while popping a huge piece of bubble gum.

"Hey, Chelle! Guess where I went last night! Paris!" Msomaji's eyes began to light up.

"Girl! What are you talking about?" Michelle said, rolling her eyes. "You know you've never been to Paris. Stop playing!"

"I did. I saw the Eiffel Tower and the Mona Lisa—well, it was all in *my dream*—but—still—" Msomaji saw the look on her friends' face and began to feel a little ashamed.

"I told you to stop all that dreaming, Msomaji! Travel ain't for people like us! Travel is for rich folks and your parents ain't nowhere near rich!"

Msomaji knew her friend didn't mean any harm. She just didn't want her to get her hopes up about something that may never happen. She turned, looked out of the window and said "One day, I'm gonna see the world. Especially Paris."

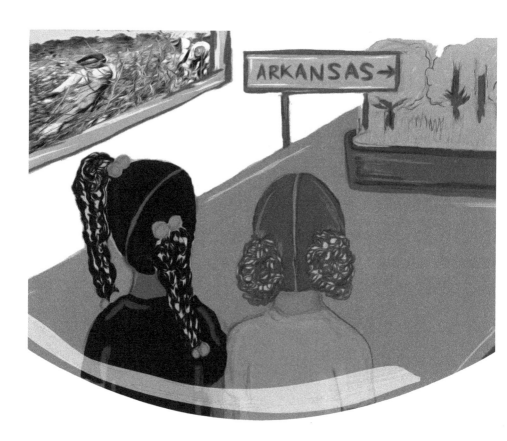

When the bus dropped them off in front of the museum, Msomaji and all of her classmates formed a single-file line and went inside. She had never been to an African American History Museum before, but she was eager to explore.

She spent the day looking around the museum, taking in all of the rich history, and learning about the contributions that African Americans have made. The museum had special exhibits for all 50 U.S. states. When Msomaji saw the area that highlighted Arkansas, she got excited.

She pointed and said "That's where my grandparents are from!" She walked over to an interactive exhibit about The "Little Rock Nine."

She listened as a voice from a speaker detailed the journey of nine Black girls that challenged the Jim Crow law of school segregation by enrolling at an all White high school in 1957. She read that even after the 1954 Brown vs. Board of Education decision, which ruled it illegal to keep Blacks and Whites separate in schools, African Americans still had to courageously fight for equal rights.

What caught her attention next, was an exhibit with old pictures of enslaved Africans standing in a cotton field. She learned all about how slaves made cotton big-business in Arkansas and the conditions they had no choice but to endure while being used as cheap labor. Her grandparents were from a small town called Cotton Plant.

At home, Msomaji's parents didn't mention much about her ancestors who were enslaved. They always made Cotton Plant seem like it was full of love, family, and great food. Msomaji's parents told her that before her grandmother passed away, she took her on a train ride to Arkansas as a baby to meet some of her relatives. She often wondered what the experience would be like if she had the chance to visit today.

"There you go *daydreaming* again," Michelle said. "Come on, girl! We gotta go!"

They walked around the museum a little longer before the teacher gathered the class and boarded everyone on the bus. Msomaji couldn't wait to get home and tell her parents what she saw at the museum.

The bus pulled up in front of her house and Msomaji barely muttered a "See ya, Chelle!" before skipping off the bus and running inside.

"Mama! Mama! Today at the museum we learned about enslaved Africans. Some of them were from Arkansas! We learned about how they picked cotton, and about sharecropping, and about the famous blues singer Rosetta Tharpe who was from Cotton Plant, and about The Little Rock Nine, and—" Msomaji's mom cut her off. "Child, please slow down! Your mouth is going a mile a minute and you haven't even taken your coat off!"

Msomaji flung her coat across the room and said, "Mama, I know that you said that Grandma took me down south when I was a baby, but maybe we can go back, especially since you have a new baby now.

I'm sure our relatives in Cotton Plant would love to meet her." Msomaji leaned over and gave her baby sister a big kiss on the forehead.

"We've been over this a million times," her mom said. "Your daddy and I just can't afford to take you and your sisters out of town. Now pick up your coat, hang it up in the closet and go upstairs and start your homework."

Msomaji felt like she had the wind knocked out of her. She walked up the stairs and into the bedroom she shared with her other sister Tajiri.

She laid on the bed and mashed her face in the pillow. "What's wrong?" Tajiri asked. "Lemme guess. Mama told you that they don't have money to take us out of town—again. I don't know why you keep asking!"

Msomaji looked up at her sister and said, "Sometimes like Dad says, you gotta *dream big* and believe that if you ask enough times, maybe it'll happen."

Tajiri shook her head and said, "Well, you've been asking for years and it still hasn't happened. So what does that tell you?"

Msomaji was frustrated. She grabbed her magic carpet, closed her eyes and imagined herself with her relatives in Arkansas sitting on the porch, laughing with family, eating her grandmother's delicious turkey and dressing and hearing the colorful stories that her grandfather used to tell while sitting in his rocking chair. Time with them always made Msomaji feel special and loved.

She wished that she could stay on her magic carpet and *daydream* forever, but she was suddenly startled by her mom's voice.

"Finish your homework, Msomaji. I'm gonna get your sister her bottle and a nap and then I'm gonna take you out to dinner someplace special." Msomaji's eyes lit up. "Just the two of us?" "Yep!" her mom replied. "Just the two of us."

Msomaji couldn't wait to see where her mom was taking her for dinner. She quickly finished her homework then eagerly hopped down the steps into the living room and over to the coat closet.

"Where are we going Mama?" she asked.

"You'll see." Her mom replied.

They hopped on a bus and after a short ride, arrived in front of a building with a large colorful awning.

"Ready to go to Africa, Msomaji?"

Msomaji looked up at her mom excitedly and yelled "Yay!"

When they walked in, a man with a distinct accent greeted them at the door.

"Welcome to **Flavors of Africa**, ladies. Let me show you to your table."

The tables had kente tablecloths with red cups and napkins and the walls were covered with paintings of Africa, along with photographs of African leaders past and present.

Msomaji sat down and said, "Mama! This is so cool! I've never had African food before! Have you?"

 "No, I haven't," she replied. "But I know that you love travel. So I wanted to show you that you don't always need to get on a plane to discover a new place."

The waiter brought the menus to the table. "Hello, I'm Yemi and I'll be your waiter."

"Hi, Yemi. What do you recommend?" Msomaji's mom asked.

"I'd recommend the Jollof rice with beef, chicken or fish," he said. "Sounds good. Give us two—with chicken. Thank you!"

"So tell me what you know about Africa, young lady." Msomaji's mom asked curiously as she ate her Jollof rice.

"I know that it's where my ancestors are from, that Nelson Mandela was South Africa's first Black president, that it's very hot there, and that it's a big, beautiful country!" Msomaji said.

"Aht, aht, aht!" Msomaji's mom sternly interrupted. "Africa is actually a continent with fifty-four countries. It is the second-largest continent in the world."
"Oh wow! So Africa is huuuuuge!" Msomaji yelled with

her arms stretched wide.

"I see this young lady is getting a lesson about Africa," Yemi said as he refilled the two cups with water.

"Yes, she is." Msomaji's mom replied. And you're just in time to tell us a little more about the food we've ordered."

"Well ladies, Jollof rice is a very popular dish in West Africa. The region consists of about sixteen countries including Ghana, Senegal and Nigeria. Jollof rice is prepared with tomatoes, onions, peppers and other spices and ingredients. The recipes vary depending on which part of West Africa you're from."

Well, this version is delicious!" Msomaji said."

"I'm glad you ladies are enjoying your meal." Yemi replied.

From the moment she walked in the house that night, Msomaji couldn't stop talking about Africa.

"Daddy, Mama and I went to Africa!"

"Well that certainly was a quick trip!" her dad replied.

"We went to an African restaurant and ate Jollof rice and chicken." Msomaji said.

"Now that sounds more realistic. An African restaurant. You got to travel a little today, eh?" Her dad looked down at her, raising his eyebrow.

"Yeah, but the real thing would be even better!" Msomaji wrapped her arms around her dad's waist and buried her head in his side, smiling. "Don't start!" Msomaji's dad said, laughing at her persistence. "Go and tell your Mama thanks for dinner and get ready for bed."

Ok, Daddy!" She replied.

Msomaji ran into the bedroom, where her mother stood looking in the mirror.

"Mama, dinner was great! Thank you for my trip to Africa," she said, hugging her mom.

"You're welcome, love. Remember, sometimes you can learn about other parts of the world without actually traveling."

"Goodnight, Mama!"

Msomaji ran up the stairs, put on her pajamas and sat on the bed. She knew that her mother was right, but it sure would be nice to actually see Africa up close, she thought. She grabbed her magic carpet, closed her eyes, and tried to imagine what all of Africa looked like—The various hues of people, the pyramids, the animals, the history and the unique traditions.

She wondered if it was even possible to one day explore a place so far away. Sometimes she wondered if she should hold onto hope of traveling at all, since it hadn't happened yet. Then she remembered her dad's voice saying *"Dream big, kid"*. She continued to imagine Africa in all of its glory until she drifted off to sleep.

Msomaji woke up the next morning excited because every Friday her class was assigned a special English project that the students would have one week to complete. Some weeks, the assignment was poetry. Other weeks, it was a short story. Msomaji loved English because it gave her a chance to express her creative side. She got dressed and ran downstairs. "Morning, Mama! It's a beautiful day!"

"Now what are you so excited about?" Msomaji's mom asked. "Oh! That's right! Mrs. Collins English class."

"Yep! I can't wait to see what our writing assignment is today! Maybe one day I'll be a famous writer. Maybe one day I'll travel and write about it. Do people make money doing that, Mama?"

"Yep. They're called travel journalists." "Oooo, yeah! Maybe, just maybe, I'll become a travel journalist!" She said.

"Now why do you keep using the word 'maybe'?" Msomaji's mom asked. "If there is something you want, you should speak those things that be not as though they were. And then, you put in the work!"

"Huh?!" Msomaji muttered, looking up at her mom.

"Child, words have power! Saying that something maybe or might happen is almost the same as saying that you have doubts about it! If you want it to come to pass, speak it like it is already done. Now say 'I am Msomaji. And I am a travel journalist.'"

Msomaji repeated her mother's words with conviction. She felt empowered on her way to school as she replayed the lesson that her mother gave her in her head. She kept saying to herself, "I am Msomaji and I am a travel journalist."

Msomaji ran into English class and grabbed her usual seat in the front next to Michelle. Mrs. Collins walked into the classroom, followed by a tall woman with dark-brown skin who wore a black suit. "Listen up everyone, Mrs. Collins began. We have a special guest with us today. This is Alicia Jones and she's going to say a few words to you before I tell you about your assignments."

Msomaji sat up straight in her seat. She couldn't wait to hear what the woman had to say.

"Hello everyone. My name is Alicia and I am a travel journalist for a national magazine. I fly all over the world to different cities and countries, and I write about the unique places that I visit."

Msomaji almost fell out of her chair. She leaned over and whispered to Michelle. "Girl! Did you hear that?! You won't believe what me and Mama talked about before school!"

"Ummm, excuse me!" Mrs. Collins interjected. "I know that one of my best students isn't being disrespectful by speaking at the same time as our guest! Would you like to share the conversation with us, Msomaji?!"

"Oh! I'm sorry Mrs. Collins and Ms. Alicia." Msomaji said. "But I am a travel journalist too!" The entire class erupted into laughter. Msomaji sank down in her seat, humiliated. She was kicking herself for saying that out loud.

"Quiet everybody!" Mrs. Collins yelled tapping on her desk.

Alicia smiled at Msomaji and walked over, reaching out to shake her hand. "I love your confidence. You'll need it in this career. So tell me about your love of travel, Msomaji."

Msomaji sat back up in her seat. Well, I love to watch travel shows and read books, and visit different restaurants and I absolutely love Paris—"

That's great! What places have you visited so far?" Alicia asked.

"No place!" A boy seated in the back yelled, causing the class to erupt into laughter again.

"Quiet!" Mrs. Collins yelled. Msomaji sank down in her seat again and said, "Well, I've never actually traveled in real life, but someday I will!"

Alicia smiled, leaned over and looked Msomaji straight in the eyes. "You absolutely will," she said.

Alicia spent another thirty minutes with Msomaji and her class answering questions about her role as a travel journalist. She talked about getting her college degree, working in a newsroom for about ten years, and then deciding to make a career out of her love of travel.

Msomaji was mesmerized. She wondered if the conversation that she'd had with her mom before school had actually played a part in her meeting Alicia.

Msomaji replayed her mom's voice in her head, remembering what she said about words having power. She wondered what else she could make happen by simply speaking and believing.

"Okay, class, it's time for this week's assignment," Mrs. Collins said. "You will write an essay about what travel means to you. It should be at least 3 pages long. And do not try and write larger to take up space on the paper, please! I want these essays to be well thought out. And just to make sure that everyone works their hardest, I have a big incentive. Alicia volunteers with an organization that sponsors trips for youth. She will choose two of the best essay writers to join her at the Young Writers of the World Conference in New Orleans, Louisiana at the end of the school year."

Msomaji' jumped out of her seat with excitement. "So we actually get to travel on a real plane?"

"That's right!" Alicia said. "An all—expenses—paid trip to New Orleans!"

Msomaji's mouth dropped open. She knew what she had to do. She was already planning to write the best essay Mrs. Collins and Alicia had ever read.

Msomaji got home, made a bee-line past her mom, and sisters, and ran straight upstairs. Her mother followed her. "Well, hello to you too! Did you not have a good day at school?"

"Mom, it was a *magical day*! You won't believe what happened!" Msomaji said excitedly. "Remember before I left, we talked about me becoming a travel journalist? Well, guess who came to Mrs. Collins class today? A real life travel journalist! I couldn't believe it! And she told us that she wants us to write an essay about what travel means to us and the winner gets a free trip to New Orleans!"

"No wonder you went straight to your room. You've got some work to do!" Msomaji's mom replied. "I've gotta win this contest!" Msomaji said with a worried look on her face.

"Now you just forgot everything we talked about this morning," her mom said, looking disappointed. "I told you that words have power! If you want it, claim it and put in the work! Nobody in that class knows travel like you do. So it's already yours. But you have to believe that."

"You're right! I'm gonna win that contest!" Msomaji said. "You sure are! Now get to work!" Msomaji's mom said, giving her a big kiss on the cheek. "I believe in you."

Msomaji took some deep breaths to calm her thoughts before writing. She closed her eyes for a second and thought of all the cool things she'd learned about New Orleans while watching one of her favorite travel shows.

She sat on her magic carpet and imagined herself tracing the steps of the indigenous tribes that originally inhabited the land and the Africans who once gathered to sing, dance and play instruments in Congo Square. She wondered what it must be like to live in Treme' and experience one of the oldest Black neighborhoods in America —taste the crawfish and beignets —hear the horns going while the second-line bands took over the streets.

She shook herself out of her daydream and focused on her essay. She grabbed her pencil and said aloud, "What does travel mean to me?" Then she wrote:

"For a little girl like me who is a dreamer at heart, travel means freedom. Sometimes we're stuck in one place. And even though that place may not be bad, it's always nice to have the freedom to see other places too. Seeing the world and learning about other cultures and different foods and languages, is something that I think makes us all better people. I don't believe we're meant to stay in one place. Education isn't just about sitting in a classroom. Seeing the world can be our teacher too ."

Msomaji continued to write until her eyes got tired and she drifted off to sleep.

The next morning was Saturday, and Msomaji always looked forward to her dad making a big breakfast for the family on Saturday's. The smell of the biscuits and bacon was almost like an alarm clock for her and Tajiri. They got up, threw on their slippers, hopped downstairs, and went straight to the kitchen.

"Mmmmm...bacon!" Msomaji said, reaching for a piece on the stove.

"Now you know better than that!" her dad said, smacking her hand away from the plate. "You and your sister go and wash your hands!"

They both quickly went to the bathroom to wash their hands and faces before returning to the kitchen to sit in front of the huge spread their dad had prepared for the family—biscuits, bacon, scrambled cheese eggs, and hash browns with green peppers and onions.

"Thanks for making breakfast, sweetie." Msomaji's mom said, giving her husband a big kiss on the cheek.

"Let's eat!" Tajiri said.
"Not before we pray," Msomaji's mom replied.
"I'll pray," Msomaji said, bowing her head.

"Dear God, we gather together today with hearts of thanksgiving. May eating this food nourish our bodies, much like how gathering with family nourishes our souls. In your name we pray, Amen."

"That was deep!" Tajiri said, grabbing the biscuits. "Let's eat! I'm starving!"

"Now, Tajiri, don't tease your sister," Msomaji's dad said, pointing his finger.

"That was an awesome prayer, Msomaji! So tell me about this contest that's gonna send you to New Orleans."

"Well, I met a travel journalist in Mrs. Collins' class, and she talked to us about what she does for a living. She works with an organization that sends kids out of town, and our class has to write about what travel means to us. The two best essays get a free trip to The Big Easy!"

"The Big Easy, huh? Sounds like you're already acquainted with the city. How's the essay coming?" her dad asked, chewing his food.

"The masterpiece is almost finished, Daddy." Msomaji replied with confidence.

"Well, I want you to know that I believe in you," her dad said. "I've always said that my children would grow up and be better than me. This one trip could be the beginning of something special for you, Msomaji. Something that could take you far!"

"I believe in you too, big sis," Tajiri said. "Your dream to travel could finally come true. Make sure you take lots of pictures!"

"Oh, she's definitely gonna win that contest," Msomaji's mom said, clearing the table.

Just write from the heart. We all believe that you can do it."

Msomaji spent the rest of the week putting all of her focus into her essay.

Friday finally came. Before she left home, Msomaji placed her essay in a special folder decorated with airplanes and clouds. Her dad bought it for her when he found out about the contest. He handed it to her and said, "This is for the writer." She thought about her dad and smiled.

Msomaji was so nervous when she arrived in Mrs. Collins class that her stomach was in knots. She took her usual seat in the classroom and shortly thereafter Mrs. Collins walked in.

"Quiet class! It's time to collect your essays on what travel means to you. I hope you all worked hard to win that contest. I will collect your papers and take them to Alicia. In one week, Alicia will join the class again to announce the winners.

"You mean we have to wait another week?" Msomaji asked nervously. "I don't think that I can wait that long!"

"Well, you'll have to," Mrs. Collins replied. "We need time to pick the winner."

Michelle leaned over and whispered, "I don't know why you're worried, girl! You know you're gonna win the contest."

Msomaji shook her head wondering how she was going to survive in suspense, waiting to find out if she'd won. She spent the next week thinking about all of the cool things she wanted to see when she arrived down south. Every night, she'd grab her *magic carpet* and dream of going to the airport, getting on the plane, flying above the clouds, and then landing in New Orleans.

Then the day finally came. It was time for Mrs. Collins and Alicia to announce the winners of the essay contest. Msomaji's stomach knotted up again when she saw them both walk into the classroom.

"Hello everyone," Mrs. Collins said. "Of course you all remember Alicia. She and I have spent the last week going over your assignments. We can tell that you all worked very hard. But we can only pick two of the best essays."

Alicia stood over Mrs. Collins' desk and pulled two essays from a manilla folder. "I was impressed with your creativity," she said. "This is truly a bright class." "I want to let you all know that whether you have the best essay or not, you should continue to work hard on your writing and stay focused. You never know where your dreams might take you someday." Msomaji began to bite her lip. She couldn't wait any longer.

"The winners are—Joshua Gray and Msomaji Mohammed."

"Yes! Yes! Yes!" Msomaji' screamed. She couldn't contain her excitement.

Michelle leaned over and said, "I told you! You deserve it, best friend," she high-fived Msomaji.

"Let's give them both a hand, class." Mrs. Collins said as she began to clap.

Msomaji and Joshua walked to the front of the class with huge grins as everyone clapped in celebration. After everyone settled down, Alicia said, "Both of your essays blew me away. And you deserve to be rewarded.

But, unfortunately, I have some bad news. The Young Writers of the World are no longer going to New Orleans."

Msomaji and Josh looked confused. Msomaji looked at Mrs. Collins and Alicia, "So I can't go to New Orleans?" She asked. "But—but I worked so hard."

"I know you did," Alicia said. "You both did, and I'm sorry." Msomaji felt tears well up in her eyes. "All that dreaming and putting in the work for nothing," she thought to herself. She felt awful.

As Msomaji and Josh headed back to their desks, Alicia said, "Before you take your seats, I want you to know that we still have very nice prizes for the both of you."

Msomaji just wanted to go home. She couldn't wait for class to be over so that she could go to the bathroom and cry.

Alicia handed Josh and Msomaji pink envelopes and said, "I think you should open them."

Msomaji was already humiliated. She didn't think she could take much more. She tried to be polite, looked up at Alicia, and said, "I'd rather not."

Alicia winked and said, "Trust me."

Msomaji flipped the pink envelope over and there was an Eiffel Tower sticker that sealed it, with the words "**DREAM BIG**" written in cursive. She was confused all over again. She broke the seal and read the letter inside:

> "The Young Writer's of the World are pleased to announce their first international conference in *Paris, France*—"

Msomaji's mouth dropped. She began to tear up again.

"Is this for real?! This can't be real!"

"Oh, it's real!" Alicia said. "You're going to Paris!"

The class began to cheer again. Msomaji stood in front of the class speechless. She felt like it was all a dream.

She thought back to when she told Michelle on the way to the museum that one day she'd see Paris. She thought about how many nights she'd spent *dreaming* about the Eiffel Tower on her magic carpet. Then she thought about how hard she worked on her essay and she heard her mother's voice: "If you want it, claim it, and put in the work."

Msomaji got home and ran through the door with the pink envelope still in hand. Her parents were sitting on the couch in the living room, watching television.

"Mama! Daddy! She yelled. You won't believe what happened in class!"

"Sounds like my girl is going to New Orleans!" her mom said with a big smile.

"No! No! Look!" she said, handing her the letter.

Her mom opened it and began to read. "Wait. This says you're going to Paris!" "Oh, baby! You worked so hard on that essay that you got an even bigger blessing than you expected! I'm so proud of you!"

"Msomaji's dad became emotional. He always wanted his girls to experience a life he never could. That's why he worked so hard. "You never cease to amaze me, kid. I told you one day you'd go. Here's to dreaming big!" he said, raising his glass.

Msomaji looked at her dad, smiled and said "No, Daddy. Here's to *dreams that come true*!"

About the Author

Tiffany D. Smith is a journalist, world traveler, mentor and foodie from Chicago, IL. After spending 16 years working in live TV News, she decided to launch The Love of Food & Travel LLC to inspire kids to see the world. She fell in love with travel after receiving her first passport stamp in her late 30's and has since become passionate about teaching kids from underserved communities the benefits of experiencing other cultures. She holds a Masters Degree in Journalism and a Bachelor's Degree in Radio & Television Production from Southern Illinois University at Carbondale.

Her work has been published in xoNecole, Blackdoctor.org and The Chicago Defender. She is also a volunteer with Chicago Public Schools and soon plans to make travel accessible to Black children by curating local and international trips. In her free time, Tiffany loves reading books on spirituality, doing yoga and spending time with family and friends.